Wh
George Lucas?

Who Is George Lucas?

By Pam Pollack and Meg Belviso
Illustrated by Ted Hammond

Grosset & Dunlap
An Imprint of Penguin Group (USA) LLC

For JR Van Deusen, who saw *Star Wars* eleven times
that summer, and his granddaughter Leia—PP

To Doug Snyder, my Jedi Knight in shining armor—MB

To my children, Stephanie and Jason—TH

GROSSET & DUNLAP
Published by the Penguin Group
Penguin Group (USA) LLC, 375 Hudson Street, New York, New York 10014, USA

USA | Canada | UK | Ireland | Australia | New Zealand | India | South Africa | China

penguin.com
A Penguin Random House Company

Library of Congress Cataloging-in-Publication Data is available.

ISBN 978-0-448-47947-7   10 9 8 7 6 5 4 3 2 1

Contents

Who Is
George Lucas?

In 1977, film director George Lucas invited some friends to his house in San Anselmo, California. He promised to show them an early, unfinished version of the new movie he was making. George had been working on *Star Wars* for eighteen hours a day for over a year.

George settled everyone in front of the screen, where they watched Luke Skywalker battling Darth Vader and the dreaded Death Star. They met the droids R2-D2 and C-3PO. They learned about the Force, the mystical power that Jedi space knights use to control the world around them.

When the movie finished, everyone was thinking the same thing: It was a disaster.

After the screening, one friend wasn't afraid to tell George what he really thought. Brian De Palma, another young director, teased him relentlessly about the "almighty Force" and the questionable wardrobe choices. "Hey, George, what were those Danish rolls doing in the princess's ears?" he asked about Princess Leia's soon-to-be-famous hairstyle. Even worse than De Palma's teasing was the pity expressed by George's other friends.

Always shy and quiet, George simply listened to the criticism.

Steven Spielberg thought the movie was good, but George had already accepted that it was a failure. "I figured, well, it's just a silly movie," he said later. "It ain't going to work."

After the screening, Alan Ladd Jr., the studio executive who had given George the money to make *Star Wars*, called Spielberg and asked him what he really thought of the movie.

"I think this film is going to make a hundred million dollars," Spielberg said. "People will love it."

Spielberg was right. People loved *Star Wars*. What he didn't know was that *Star Wars* would become much more than a hit movie. It would forever change the way movies were made.

Chapter 1
Ramona Avenue

On May 14, 1944, George Walton Lucas Jr.
was born in Modesto, California. His father,
George Sr., and his mother, Dorothy, already
had two daughters, Ann and Katy. When George

was three, his younger sister, Wendy, was born into the growing family on Ramona Avenue.

As a young boy, George often ran errands for his father's stationery store after school, but he wasn't interested in greeting cards and writing paper. What George loved was listening to radio shows and picturing everything in his mind. He loved comic books like *Scrooge McDuck* and pulp magazines like *Amazing Stories*. When the

family got their first television, George was ten.
He devoured new shows like *Have Gun Will
Travel* and *Gunsmoke*. He also watched old serials
on TV—serials were short movies that always
ended on a cliffhanger with the hero in danger.
George loved wondering what would happen next.

To George, the stories in his head were more
interesting than the things he was studying in
school, and his grades showed it. His father
wasn't happy with his report cards, but George's

imagination was too big to control. He was
always making plans. With the help of his sister
Wendy and his best friends, John Plummer and
George Frankenstein, he organized a backyard
carnival with rides and games, a homemade fun

house, and a zoo filled with all the pets in the
neighborhood.

At the center of the carnival was a roller coaster that George designed. It rolled down an incline, rotated on a turntable made out of a huge telephone-wire spool, and rolled onto the ground.

George also liked building "environments"— tiny worlds, cities, and farms made of dirt, berries, and cement poured into carefully made molds.

When George had an idea, it could be amazing.

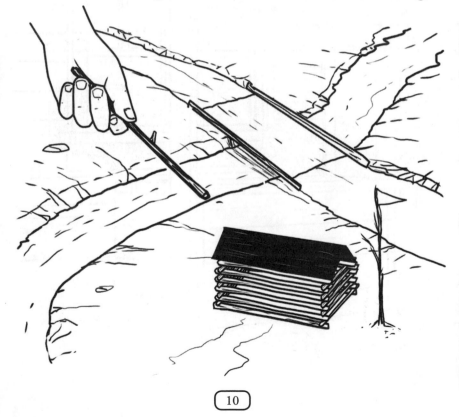

When George was eleven, his family traveled
to Anaheim, California, for the opening of
Disneyland. Disneyland was like one of George's
environments on a grand scale, a whole world built
from the imagination of one man, Walt Disney.

George Sr. thought practical things, like earning money, were more important than imagination. All the Lucas children worked hard for a weekly allowance. One of George's chores was mowing the lawn with the manual mower. He was so small he couldn't do it well. If only they had an electric lawn mower, he could do his chores more quickly and efficiently. But electric lawn mowers were expensive. For four months George saved every penny of his allowance. That gave him $35—still not enough for a lawn mower. He borrowed another $25 from his mother and bought a power mower for $60.

George Sr. was furious that George didn't ask permission. But as he watched the boy cutting the grass more smoothly than he ever had before, he felt a strange kind of pride. George was stubborn. He did things the way he wanted to do them. But his father couldn't deny that the lawn mower was a smart idea.

In his own way, his imaginative son was also a good businessman.

Chapter 2
Cruising

When George was fifteen, his family moved from Ramona Avenue to a walnut ranch on the outskirts of Modesto. There was plenty of room for George to pursue his new passions. The first was music. When school was over, rather than doing his homework, George locked himself in his room, listening to rock and roll, drinking Coca-Cola, and eating Hershey bars.

George's father bought him a 35-millimeter camera and helped him convert the family's spare bathroom into a darkroom to develop pictures. Whenever George heard a crop plane flying overhead, he ran outside to take pictures of it.

THE BIRTH OF ROCK AND ROLL

ROCK AND ROLL WAS BORN OUT OF THE TRADITIONS OF COUNTRY MUSIC, RHYTHM AND BLUES, AND GOSPEL MUSIC. AFTER WORLD WAR II, WITH THE GROWING AVAILABILITY AND MASS PRODUCTION OF RECORD PLAYERS,

ELECTRIC GUITARS, AND TRANSISTOR RADIOS, SONGS LIKE "ROCK AROUND THE CLOCK" BY BILL HALEY AND THE COMETS, "THAT'S ALL RIGHT" BY ELVIS PRESLEY, AND "MAYBELLENE"

BY CHUCK BERRY GAINED POPULARITY. THE ROCK-AND-ROLL SOUND HAD A DRIVING BEAT AND A FAST TEMPO THAT KIDS LOVED AND PARENTS HATED.

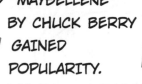

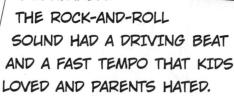

MORE THAN JUST A STYLE OF MUSIC, ROCK AND ROLL BECAME A LOOK AND AN ATTITUDE, INFLUENCING FASHION AND LANGUAGE. IT WAS EXCITING, REBELLIOUS, AND WILD.

When he was fourteen, George became
fascinated with motorcycles. A year later, his
focus shifted to cars. He was still too young to
have a license, but he often drove around the
ranch for fun. He hung out in auto repair shops,
looking under the hoods of cars. At sixteen,

George failed his driver's test because he didn't follow the rules of the road. He eventually got his license, but he still wasn't good at following the rules. George Sr. also got George his own car, a Fiat. It wasn't the kind of car George had in mind. "It had a sewing machine motor in it," he said. "It was a dumb little car. What could I do with that? It was practically a motor scooter." George made plans to turn the Fiat into a racing car.

George's parents were getting worried. His grades were terrible. He looked like a JD—juvenile delinquent. Nice boys in the late 1950s wore chinos and sweaters and cut their hair short. George grew his hair past his ears and slicked it back with Vaseline. He wore dirty jeans and white T-shirts. George was becoming a greaser (so named for all the grease they wore in their hair).

George and his friends drove up and down the

streets of Modesto looking for girls and listening
to rock and roll. George's favorite radio DJ was
Wolfman Jack, the outlaw of the airwaves, who
broadcast late at night from a Mexican radio
station. No one knew the real identity of the
Wolfman, but George came to think of him as a
friend.

George and his friends called what they did at night "cruising." They drove the same circuit over and over, around Tenth and Eleventh Streets. On the way they talked to kids in other cars and switched passengers—it was a giant party on the road every night. Occasionally they raced each other.

In the afternoons, George beefed up the engine of his Fiat at the local garage. The car was getting

faster. George loved taking corners at top speed,
enjoying the feel of being *almost* out of control.
One afternoon he skidded and rolled the car over.
It didn't slow George down. He just cut off the
dented roof and replaced it with a roll bar—a
tubular bar meant to protect passengers if the car
flipped over.

George longed to be a race-car driver. He
couldn't enter Formula One races until he was
twenty-one, but he won a lot of trophies in
autocrosses, competitions held in parking lots. He
joined a sports-car competition club and edited its
newsletter.

George's boyhood
friends like John
Plummer had been nice
kids. His new friends
were greasers.
John Plummer
called them "the
undesirables
and low-riders
of town." George

was the smallest kid in his class, but he had tough
friends like a local gang in black leather jackets
called the Faros.

This was not what George Sr. had in mind for
his son. He had always thought George would one
day inherit his stationery store. He gave him a job
working at the store, but George hated hauling
the heavy boxes of paper and sweeping the floor.
When George told his father he didn't want to
go into the family business, they had a big fight.

"I'm going to be a millionaire before I'm thirty," George declared before storming out.

George's high-school graduation was approaching, but it didn't look like he would pass. With three days of school left, on June 12, 1962, George went to the library to study. Speeding home around 5:00 p.m., he made a left turn onto the dirt road that led to his house. He heard a frantic honking and the roar of an engine and then—*CRASH*! Another car hit George broadside. The Fiat flew into the air and flipped over five or six times before wrapping itself around a walnut tree that was ripped right out of the ground.

George's seat belt snapped on impact. He was thrown out of the car. He lay in the road in a pool of blood.

When the ambulance arrived they could barely hear a heartbeat.

Chapter 3
Star Student

George woke up in the hospital with tubes in his arms, needles in his stomach, and an oxygen tube up his nose. He could barely see his mother beside him. "Mom," he whispered, "did I do something wrong?" Dorothy started to weep.

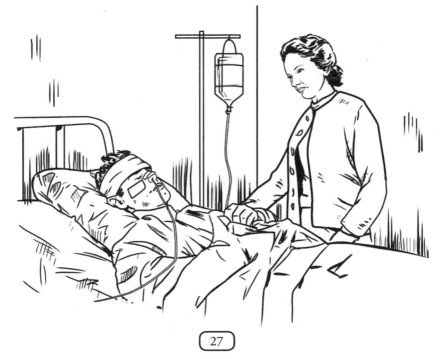

Had he not been thrown out of the car, George would have died. During his two weeks in the hospital and the long recovery afterward, he changed his mind about being a race-car driver. Now he wanted to do something meaningful with his life.

He missed his final exams, but Thomas Downey High School awarded him a diploma

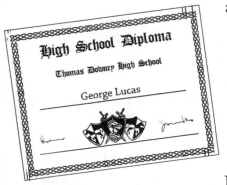

anyway. Little did they know the former greaser was making plans for college. When he was well enough, George enrolled in Modesto Junior College and studied sociology, anthropology, literature, and astronomy. For the first time, George became a great student. Soon he was ready to move on to a four-year college.

John Plummer encouraged George to apply

to the University of Southern California in Los Angeles. Haskell Wexler was a Hollywood cinematographer who knew George through the racing circuit. He offered to help George. The film school at USC was top-notch. George had always loved photography. Now he wanted to make movies. George Sr. wasn't happy about the idea—it didn't sound very practical—but he agreed to pay the tuition.

George arrived at USC in 1964. The school's motto was "Reality Stops Here." It meant that anything was possible, that dreams started there.

At USC, George studied English, astronomy, history of film and animation, and drama. He knew he had found his calling. He made his first short film, *Look at Life*, in 1965. George quickly became part of the elite group of students who were considered the best in the class. He and his friends edited films at night because they were allowed only two hours a day on the Moviola editing machine. George loved cutting

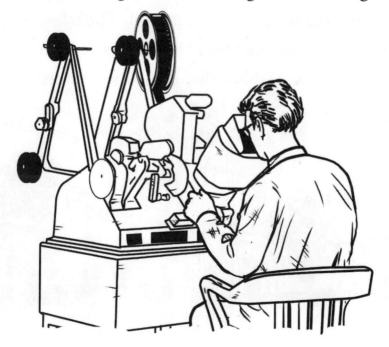

shots together to make meaning out of pictures. Through editing he could conceal some of his weaknesses as a beginning filmmaker. He didn't yet understand how to write strong characters or work with actors to bring about better performances.

Student films at USC were shown in public screenings. George's family came from Modesto to see his. George Sr. noticed that any time one of George's films came up, the "long-haired hippie kids" in the audience whispered, "Watch this one, it's George's film!" He said to his wife, "I think we put our money on the right horse." Once again George had surprised him.

George graduated from USC on August 6, 1966, at twenty-two. He hoped to make documentaries—films that present actual events and facts, rather than made-up stories—or to become a cameraman. But young men George's age were being drafted to fight in the Vietnam

War. However, during his army physical he found out that he was diabetic. He could not be in the military. He could also no longer wash down chocolate bars with sugary soda. He returned to USC to attend graduate school in 1967. To pay his way he became a teacher's assistant. At this time, the cinematography department had a contract to teach US Navy cameramen. George was assigned to teach the class in the evenings—and he got extra color film to make his own movies.

During the day he worked for Verna Fields, a top-notch editor, on a film about President Lyndon Johnson's visit to Asia. The government wanted the film to make the president look good. Any shot that showed Johnson's bald spot was cut. George hated other people telling him what to do. "I really wanted to be responsible for what was being said in a movie," he said later.

George really liked Verna Fields's assistant, Marcia Griffin. Marcia was a talented editor

MARCIA GRIFFIN

who fought her way into the male-dominated industry as an assistant. George had never had a real girlfriend, but he and Marcia soon began dating.

While teaching at night, George shot his own films during the day. His biggest project was *Electronic Labyrinth: THX 1138 4EB*, the story of a man in a futuristic world. George called it a "science fiction documentary." He recruited half his navy class as his crew. They were fascinated by his story of what life might be like in the future. It was a smash at student screenings. Aspiring filmmakers from all over California came to see it, including one from Long Beach State named Steven Spielberg.

In the late 1960s and early 1970s, Hollywood was changing. George Lucas was one of a group of young film directors in New York and Los Angeles who were more daring and more experimental about the way they made movies. They helped each other, inspired each other, and competed with each other to make the best movies they could. To the businessmen who had ruled Hollywood for decades, they were just kids.

Yet they were creating amazing films that were
changing the way people thought about movies.

At the National Student Film Festival in
1967, *Electronic Labyrinth: THX 1138 4EB*
won the dramatic prize, and two other films by
George won honorable mentions. He received
a scholarship to Warner Bros. and was given a
job helping another director at the studio. This

was his chance to learn more about professional filmmaking. George Lucas had conquered the student film world. Now he was going to see what Hollywood was all about.

NEW HOLLYWOOD

STEVEN SPIELBERG STUDIED AT CALIFORNIA STATE UNIVERSITY, LONG BEACH. HE CREATED THE "SUMMER BLOCKBUSTER" IN 1975 WITH HIS MOVIE *JAWS*, THE STORY OF A SEASIDE TOWN MENACED BY A GREAT WHITE SHARK, WHICH BECAME THE TOP-GROSSING FILM IN HISTORY UP TO THAT TIME. HE LATER CREATED CLASSIC SCIENCE FICTION MOVIES LIKE *CLOSE ENCOUNTERS OF THE THIRD KIND* AND *E.T.*, AND AFTER THAT, POWERFUL HISTORICAL DRAMAS LIKE *SCHINDLER'S LIST*, *SAVING PRIVATE RYAN*, AND *LINCOLN*.

STEVEN SPIELBERG

MARTIN SCORSESE WENT TO NEW YORK UNIVERSITY. HE ELECTRIFIED AUDIENCES WITH MOVIES SET ON THE MEAN STREETS OF NEW YORK WHERE HE HAD GROWN UP. HIS MOVIES INCLUDE *RAGING BULL* (1980), *GOODFELLAS* (1990), AND *THE DEPARTED* (2006).

MARTIN SCORSESE

FRANCIS FORD COPPOLA

FRANCIS FORD COPPOLA GRADUATED FROM THE UNIVERSITY OF CALIFORNIA, LOS ANGELES. HE WAS GEORGE'S MENTOR AND FRIEND. HIS FILMS *THE GODFATHER* (1972) AND *THE GODFATHER: PART II* (1974) EARNED HIM A WELL-DESERVED REPUTATION AS A MASTER FILMMAKER. *APOCALYPSE NOW* (1979), SET IN VIETNAM AND BASED ON AN IDEA GEORGE HAD BACK AT USC, IS NOW CONSIDERED BY MANY TO BE ONE OF THE BEST FILMS EVER MADE.

BRIAN DE PALMA ATTENDED COLUMBIA UNIVERSITY IN NEW YORK CITY. HE BECAME FAMOUS FOR THRILLERS LIKE *SISTERS* (1973), *CARRIE* (1976), AND *DRESSED TO KILL* (1980). HE WENT ON TO MAKE BIG-BUDGET HITS LIKE *SCARFACE* (1983), *THE UNTOUCHABLES* (1987), AND *MISSION: IMPOSSIBLE* (1996).

BRIAN DE PALMA

At Warner Bros., George was assigned to work on a movie called *Finian's Rainbow*. The director was Francis Ford Coppola. Coppola was a hero to Lucas. He was five years older and a UCLA graduate. Coppola noticed the "skinny kid" watching him, and the two became friends.

Unlike George, Coppola was big, lively, and loud. But George found the movie they were working on boring. He decided to hunt down unguarded film stock to use for a movie of his own. "What do you mean you're leaving? Aren't I entertaining enough?" Coppola demanded.

"There's nothing to do here," George said. Coppola promised to find him something to do. The two argued about *Finian's Rainbow*, but Coppola would often give in, saying, "You're a stinky kid, do what you want!" George loved the work enough to work with Coppola on his next movie, too—*The Rain People*, filmed in New York. Marcia had editing jobs elsewhere. He missed her. When she came to visit him, he asked her to marry him.

Coppola wanted to make George's student film *Electronic Labyrinth: THX 1138 4EB* into a longer film. He made a deal with Warner Bros. He would bring the studio new ideas, and Warner Bros. would pay him to develop them into movies. George got $15,000 to write a new script for *THX 1138* and direct it. Coppola and George then created their own company, called American Zoetrope, to develop and produce the film.

american zoetrope

George married Marcia on February 22, 1969. They moved to Mill Valley, California, and Marcia found work as an editor. George got to work on *THX 1138*. The first step, he thought, was to hire a writer. But Coppola said if George was going to make it in the movie business, he had to learn to write himself. George worked on the script with his USC friend Walter Murch, who would also do sound for the film.

Unlike Coppola, who spent money freely, George planned on a strict budget for *THX 1138*. He had ten weeks to shoot—the same time it took to make his short (fifteen-minute) student film version—beginning September 22, 1969. Rather than build sets, he found places in San Francisco that could pass for a landscape of the future. The movie's final chase scene took place in the half-completed train tunnels for the new Bay Area Rapid Transit system. The actors wore simple

costumes and little makeup, and they shaved their heads—even the women. Walter Murch created a "sound montage," a collection of noises and voices that played instead of music.

George edited the footage at his house in Mill Valley. In the middle of 1970, Coppola showed it to the Warner Bros. producers.

They hated it and wanted to break their whole deal with Zoetrope.

But Warner Bros. did release the film on March 11, 1971. *THX 1138* wasn't a hit. Warner refused to make any other movies with American Zoetrope.

Francis Ford Coppola and George Lucas's plans for American Zoetrope were finished.

Chapter 5
Graffiti Gamble

With Zoetrope gone, George formed his own
company, Lucasfilm Ltd. He considered trying to
write a screenplay about the Vietnam War called
Apocalypse Now. But in 1971 no one was interested
in producing a movie about the war in Vietnam.
So George put that idea on hold. Instead, he
began working on a movie about his own teenage
years. He'd loved driving up and down the streets
of Modesto. Maybe movie audiences would be

interested in a story about cruising. He called it *American Graffiti.*

If he was going to make a pitch to a studio, he needed more than one idea. As a kid, he had loved science fiction comics. Maybe he could do an exciting action movie set in space. He sent both ideas to the movie studios. Many people in Hollywood who were twice George's age and had far more experience had never even had one of their ideas picked up by a major studio. But George was confident that his could be hits.

Would anyone in Hollywood agree with him?

On George's twenty-sixth birthday, David Picker of United Artists offered him a two-picture deal if George would turn in a full screenplay for *American Graffiti*, for which they'd pay $10,000. George asked a film school friend, Richard Walter, to write the script.

But George was disappointed with Walter's script. Walter had written a movie about wild teenagers—not the movie that George had envisioned.

Now George had to write the script himself—for free, since Walter got all the money for his draft. George wrote furiously, listening to the rock-and-roll songs of his youth that he planned to use on the sound track of the movie. He borrowed money from his father and even turned down a studio directing job. Even though he needed the money, he wanted to work on his own stories.

The studio hated George's first script and turned it down.

He rewrote it and showed it to other studios. Finally Universal Pictures showed interest, but only if George could attach a famous name to the project—a famous name that audiences would recognize.

Francis Ford Coppola was famous now. After Zoetrope folded, he took a job directing the movie version of the best-selling novel *The Godfather*.

(George had assisted him, filming some scenes himself.) The movie became one of the biggest hits of 1972. So when George convinced Coppola to produce *American Graffiti*, Universal gave the go-ahead for the film.

George's friends Bill Huyck and Gloria Katz wrote the screenplay, a coming-of-age story about one night in the lives of four young men. The characters were mostly based on different aspects of George's personality. Terry the Toad was the young, awkward George. John was the drag racer. Curt

was the boy who leaves his hometown. The fourth boy, Steve, was the class president. The Faros gang members also became characters in the movie, and Wolfman Jack appeared in the film as himself.

George shot the film quickly over twenty-eight nights.

He then edited a version to show to movie executives along with a test audience. The test audience loved it—the studio hated it. "It's unreleasable!" a Universal representative said to George and Coppola. "You let me down."

George was in shock. Coppola was enraged. "You should get down on your knees . . . ! This kid has killed himself to make this movie for you. The least you can do is thank him!" Coppola then offered to buy the movie back from the studio.

George was devastated at the studio's reaction. He got angry when Universal demanded that changes be made before they would release the film. "They were simply coming in and putting a crayon mark on my painting and saying, 'Hey, don't worry about it. It's just a crayon mark.'" He vowed never to give up control of a movie again.

On August 1, 1973, *American Graffiti* was finally released. It was nominated for five Academy Awards, including Best Director and

Best Screenplay. The little movie that cost only $775,000 to make earned over $118 million.

George was generous with the cast and crew, giving them a percentage of the profits. He himself was now a millionaire, just as he'd promised his father—two years ahead of schedule!

Chapter 6
That Science Movie

When United Artists turned down *American Graffiti*, they also turned down George's space story, now called *Star Wars*. They weren't alone. So did every other studio. No one in Hollywood knew what to make of *Star Wars*. The first sentence of the story treatment was enough to confuse anyone: "the story of Mace Windu, a revered Jedi-bendu of Opuchi who was related to Usby C. J. Thape, padawaan learner to the famed Jedi."

ALAN LADD JR.

Huh?

Alan Ladd Jr. at Twentieth Century Fox

encouraged George to edit the story, and they made a deal for *Star Wars* in May 1973. *Graffiti* was released in August. By November it was a huge hit. But rather than use his new power to demand more money for *Star Wars*, George stuck to the original terms of the deal. However, he did request sequel and television rights, and rights to the merchandising (the products and toys based on the movie) and sound tracks (music used in the movie). George wanted to control his vision. The studio couldn't believe their luck—what kind of merchandise could *Star Wars* inspire? They were happy to hand control of those rights over to George.

George and Marcia moved to San Anselmo, California. Their Victorian house was also the headquarters of Lucasfilm. While Marcia edited movies for director Martin Scorsese, George worked on his script for *Star Wars*. It was inspired by the stories he loved as a child and the myths

he'd studied in college classes. Nobody else could write it.

For eight hours a day, five days a week, George locked himself in his room to write draft after draft on yellow pads of paper. He carried a notebook to jot down ideas. When filming *THX*

1138, Walter Murch had once referred to a sound tape labeled *Reel 2, Dialogue 2* as "R2-D2." George gave the name to a droid character. One day Marcia drove home with their Alaskan Malamute, Indiana, in the passenger seat of her car, inspiring the character of Han Solo's hairy copilot, Chewbacca.

ALEC GUINNESS

Finally, in March 1976, George was ready to begin shooting in the North African country of Tunisia and in England. The cast were all unknown actors except for British actor Alec Guinness, who played Obi-Wan Kenobi. George planned for the movie to have great special effects. But he wanted to create and control them. So he had hired his own team, led by John Dykstra, and set everyone up in a warehouse in Van Nuys, California. He had named the group Industrial Light and Magic, known as ILM.

George had promised Fox he'd try to make
the movie for $3.5 million, but imagined it would
cost closer to $8.5 million. The actors who played
nonhuman parts often had trouble with their
costumes. Actor Kenny Baker kept falling over
inside the R2-D2 costume. Anthony Daniels
had trouble walking as C-3PO. Peter Mayhew as
Chewbacca had to spend twelve hours a day in a
body suit made of angora wool and yak hair.

The rest of the cast had trouble with the dialogue. Harrison Ford, who played Han Solo, complained that you could *type* lines like his, but you couldn't say them. It didn't help that George didn't particularly like working with actors.

His direction mostly consisted of three phrases: "Faster and more intense," "Let's do it again, only this time do it better," or "Terrific." Just before filming began, George changed the name of his hero from Luke Starkiller to Luke Skywalker.

The shoot went over schedule and over budget. George was exhausted. He finally finished in July 1976. He visited ILM hoping to see many completed special effects. Instead ILM had used up half the budget and had completed only three shots! That night George had what he thought was a heart attack. It turned out his chest pains were the result of stress. But he went right back to work, adding the long-awaited special effects from ILM and fixing scenes in the editing room. The studio decided to release "that science movie" in only thirty-two movie theaters around the country instead of the usual six to eight hundred. They worried that no one would want to see a movie about spaceships, aliens, and robots.

George was so stressed he didn't even remember the date of the film's premiere! On May 25, 1977, he and Marcia were stuck in a traffic jam on Hollywood Boulevard as they were heading out to dinner. The street was packed with traffic. On the sidewalk, lines eight people wide stretched around the block.

"What's going on here?" George asked, peering at the crowds. Inching closer, he saw all those

people were going to Grauman's Chinese Movie
Theater. The movie title on the marquee?

STAR WARS.

Chapter 7
George Lucas Strikes Back

The very next day, George and Marcia went to
Hawaii for their first vacation since 1969. They
were joined by friends, including Steven Spielberg.
George and Steven built a sand castle and talked
about George's new idea for a film about an
archeologist who did "all kinds of neat stuff."

George named him Indiana Smith, after his dog Indiana. The two men vowed to make the movie together.

Although *Star Wars* had consumed George's life for over a year, the rest of the world had just discovered it. And they couldn't get enough. *Star Wars* won five Academy Awards, including one for its editor, Marcia. It also won awards for art direction, costume design, musical score, and special effects. George's father was stunned.

Suddenly the deal George made with the studio to retain the sequel rights and most of the merchandising rights seemed like genius.

George could have let the studio pay for the sequel they now wanted so badly. But studio money meant studio control. He decided to fund *The Empire Strikes Back* himself. Even with all his money, this was a huge risk. "It has to be the biggest-grossing sequel of all time for me to break even," he said, but he did it anyway. When executives at Twentieth Century Fox demanded to know who would write, star, and direct *Empire*, George answered, "None of your business." If the movie succeeded, George hoped to build the kind of creative retreat for filmmakers that he and Coppola had dreamed about for American Zoetrope.

George decided not to direct *Empire* himself. That job went to Irwin Kershner. George wrote a rough draft of the screenplay, then passed it on to

CHRISTMAS 1977: EMPTY BOXES

NO ONE EVER EXPECTED STAR WARS TO BE AS POPULAR AS IT IS TODAY. IN 1977, KENNER, THE TOY  COMPANY THAT HAD CONTRACTED TO MAKE THE FIRST ACTION FIGURES OF THE MOVIE CHARACTERS, COULD NOT PRODUCE THE TOYS IN TIME FOR CHRISTMAS. THEY WERE TAKEN BY SURPRISE BY THE HUGE DEMAND FOR *STAR WARS*-THEMED GIFTS. THE COMPANY ACTUALLY SHIPPED EMPTY BOXES TO TOY STORES IN TIME FOR CHRISTMAS. THE PACKAGE CAME WITH A CARDBOARD DISPLAY STAND, A FEW STICKERS, AND AN "EARLY

 BIRD" CERTIFICATE. KIDS WOULD FILL OUT THEIR CERTIFICATES, MAIL THEM IN TO KENNER, AND WAIT (MONTHS!) FOR THE ACTION FIGURES TO ARRIVE IN THE MAIL. THE SET INCLUDED FOUR FIGURES: LUKE SKYWALKER, PRINCESS LEIA, R2-D2, AND CHEWBACCA. THESE EARLY TOYS WERE SOON JOINED BY MANY MORE, BUT THE EARLY BIRD SET HAD THE DISTINCTION OF BEING THE FIRST *STAR WARS* TOYS EVER, AND THOUSANDS WERE SOLD WITH JUST A PROMISE IN AN EMPTY BOX.

Lawrence Kasdan to polish it. Instead of the hot deserts of Tunisia, the crew shot in snowy Finse, Norway. There were new gadgets and creatures to struggle with. Mark Hamill, who played Luke Skywalker, joked that all his scenes were with robots and puppets.

Even though he wasn't directing the movie,
George was working long hours. He and Marcia
hoped to start a family soon, but right now,
he didn't have much time to spend at home.
Sometimes it seemed as if Marcia was always
waiting for George.

SKYWALKER SOUND

"SOUND IS FIFTY PERCENT OF THE MOTION PICTURE EXPERIENCE," GEORGE LUCAS SAID. *THX 1138* AND *AMERICAN GRAFFITI* WERE BOTH PRAISED FOR THEIR CREATIVE USE OF SOUND EFFECTS AND MUSIC. *STAR WARS* SOUND DESIGNER BEN BURTT USED MANY DIFFERENT TYPES OF RECORDINGS TO BRING GEORGE'S WORLD TO LIFE. R2-D2'S VOICE IS A COMBINATION OF ELECTRIC BEEPS, WATER PIPES, WHISTLES, AND BURTT'S OWN VOICE. CHEWBACCA'S WOOKIEE SOUND IS A MIX OF ANGRY WALRUSES, LIONS, AND CAMELS! THE WORLD-FAMOUS LIGHTSABER SOUND EFFECT WAS CREATED IN PART BY THE HUM OF OLD MOVIE PROJECTORS. *STAR WARS* HAD CREATED A DEMAND FOR SOPHISTICATED DOLBY SOUND IN THEATERS. IN 1987, SPROCKET SYSTEMS CHANGED ITS NAME TO SKYWALKER SOUND AND INVENTED THE THX SYSTEM, WHICH IMPROVED THE SOUND QUALITY IN THEATERS EVEN MORE.

BEN BURTT

ILM was hard at work on the special visual effects. George's sound division, Sprocket Systems, worked on sound.

Empire was released on May 21, 1980—and became the most successful sequel of its time.

Again, George shared the profits generously with his cast and crew.

His professional life was going well. And his family was expanding: In 1981, George and Marcia adopted a daughter, Amanda. Marcia was eager to retire and become a full-time mom.

George was eager to get to work on his new movie.

Chapter 8
Beginnings and Endings

HARRISON FORD

While George was making *Empire*, a script was written for the movie that George and Steven Spielberg had talked about while on vacation in Hawaii: *Raiders of the Lost Ark*. It would star Harrison Ford. Famous for his role of Han Solo in *Star Wars*, Ford would play the archeologist-adventurer now called Indiana Jones.

Just as *Star Wars* was based on the Flash Gordon serials George loved as a kid, *Raiders* was based on the adventure serials made at the same time. Spielberg would direct the movie, and ILM

would create the special effects. As executive producer, George oversaw the production and was sometimes called in to solve problems.

One day Spielberg showed George a model of a German airplane he needed in one scene. It had two engines on each side. "The plane is going to cost a million dollars to build," one of the other producers said. "It's too much. What can we do?"

George picked up the model. He broke one engine off each side. Problem solved.

Raiders was another amazing hit. Everyone loved "the man in the hat": whip-cracking, wisecracking Dr. Indiana Jones. The success of *Raiders* gave George the freedom to start planning his creative headquarters, which he would call Skywalker Ranch. He'd bought 1,700 acres of land in Lucas Valley, California. (The valley was named for an early California settler who was no relation to George.) George spun a history for the ranch, starting with an imaginary railroad tycoon in the nineteenth century who built a Victorian-style house, then added stables and a library. He gave the story to the architects to inspire their plans for the buildings. It was a lot like the environments he imagined and built as a kid back in Modesto.

IT'S ALL IN THE FAMILY

GEORGE'S MOVIES OFTEN CONTAIN VISUAL CLUES AND REFERENCES TO HIS OTHER MOVIES AND HIS FRIENDS.

AMERICAN GRAFFITI

JOHN MILNER'S CAR LICENSE PLATE READS THX-138.

A MOVIE THEATER MARQUEE ADVERTISES FRANCIS FORD COPPOLA'S DEMENTIA 13.

RAIDERS OF THE LOST ARK

THE REGISTRATION CODE ON JOCK LINDSEY'S AIRPLANE IS OB-CPO.

R2-D2 AND C-3PO APPEAR AS HIEROGLYPHS IN THE WELL OF SOULS.

DURING A CLIMACTIC STANDOFF, INDY STOOD AT THE SAME SPOT IN TUNISIA WHERE R2-D2 WAS CAPTURED BY JAWAS IN STAR WARS. THE AREA WAS SUBSEQUENTLY RENAMED STAR WARS CANYON.

INDIANA JONES AND THE TEMPLE OF DOOM

A NIGHTCLUB INDY VISITS IN SHANGHAI, CHINA, IS CALLED CLUB OBI WAN.

INDIANA JONES AND THE LAST CRUSADE

INDY AND HIS FATHER COME ACROSS A PICTURE OF THE LOST ARK OF THE COVENANT FROM *RAIDERS OF THE LOST ARK*.

INDIANA JONES AND THE KINGDOM OF THE CRYSTAL SKULL

INDY SAYS, "I HAVE A BAD FEELING ABOUT THIS," JUST LIKE HAN SOLO IN *STAR WARS*.

INSIDE THE TEMPLE OF AKATOR, C-3PO AND R2-D2 CAN BE SEEN AS GOLDEN IDOL FACES.

STAR WARS: EPISODE I—THE PHANTOM MENACE

THREE REPRESENTATIVES IN THE GALACTIC SENATE RESEMBLE STEVEN SPIELBERG'S ALIEN E.T. (IN THAT MOVIE, E.T. MEETS A CHILD DRESSED AS YODA AND TRIES TO EAT A TOY BOBA FETT.)

While contractors were working hard to build their ranch, Marcia had hoped to take a vacation with George and Amanda. But George had to start work on the final movie of the Star Wars trilogy, *Revenge of the Jedi*. Although he had hired a new director, Richard Marquand, and Lawrence Kasdan had agreed to cowrite the screenplay, George still spent almost every day on the movie set.

The movie was released on May 25, 1983, exactly six years after *Star Wars*. After movie posters had already been printed, George decided to change the title from *Revenge of the Jedi* to *Return of the Jedi*, because the honorable Jedi Knights would never seek revenge. (The original *Revenge* posters are now collector's items.) *Jedi* was even more successful than *Empire*, earning over $309 million in the United States alone.

The original Star Wars trilogy was not the only thing coming to an end. Marcia had waited and waited for George to cut down on his working hours, but he always seemed to find more things to do. They grew further and further apart. Marcia stopped believing that George would pay as much attention to his marriage as he did to his movies. Shortly after the release of *Jedi*, they announced that they were getting a divorce.

MARCIA LUCAS

FEW PEOPLE KNOW OF THE MANY CONTRIBUTIONS MARCIA LUCAS MADE TO THE FILM INDUSTRY. AS AN EDITOR SHE WORKED ON SUCH CLASSIC MOVIES AS *STAR WARS* (FOR WHICH SHE WON AN OSCAR), *TAXI DRIVER*, AND *THE CANDIDATE*. SHE DID MORE THAN EDIT GEORGE'S EARLY FILMS LIKE *AMERICAN GRAFFITI* AND THE STAR WARS TRILOGY—SHE ALSO GAVE HIM GREAT ADVICE. STEVEN SPIELBERG CREDITED HER FOR SAVING THE END OF *RAIDERS OF THE LOST ARK*. IN THE ORIGINAL ENDING, INDY DELIVERS THE ARK TO THE US GOVERNMENT ALONE. AFTER AN EARLY SCREENING, MARCIA ASKED WHY MARION RAVENWOOD WAS EXCLUDED FROM THE FINAL SCENE. HAD INDY LEFT HER BEHIND? SPIELBERG TOOK MARCIA'S ADVICE AND RESHOT THE ENDING TO INCLUDE MARION.

Chapter 9
Back to the Ranch

George retreated to the new Skywalker Ranch. The ranch had a huge library under a stained-glass dome that housed thousands of films and TV shows in different formats. It contained a

collection of press clippings, ticket stubs, pictures, scripts, music scores, and production reports— over a hundred years of movie history. All of George's companies moved to Skywalker Ranch, which grew to 4,000 acres.

George loved being a father to young Amanda. He adopted another daughter, Katie, born in 1988, and a son, Jett, born in 1993. Now that

George was a father of three, he thought a lot about his own childhood. He'd spent much of it bored in school. He founded the Lucas Educational Foundation in 1991, to find ways to educate children through entertainment.

In 1992, George produced *The Young Indiana Jones Chronicles* for television. The series starred Indiana as a young boy and a teenager. He traveled the world meeting famous people and witnessing history. Carrie Fisher, who played Princess Leia in the Star Wars trilogy, wrote an episode; Harrison Ford appeared in another.

Hollywood honored George with the prestigious Irving G. Thalberg Memorial Award in 1992, three months after George Sr. died. It was presented by Steven Spielberg, who had won in 1986. George thanked his many teachers and friends, especially Coppola, saying, "Thank you, Francis, for being my mentor."

In 1994, Lucasfilm's ILM division created effects for *Jurassic Park*, a movie directed by Steven Spielberg about dinosaurs being "reborn" in the modern world. *Jurassic Park* was a turning point in moviemaking technology. The film is

regarded as a landmark in its use of computer-generated imagery. According to George, the first time he showed test footage of the textured, breathing dinosaurs to Steven and the crew, "everyone had tears in their eyes."

Looking at the dinosaurs made George think about the special effects he had dreamed of putting in *Star Wars* back in 1977. Technology and the effects wizards at ILM had finally caught up with George's imagination.

He was ready to make a new Star Wars film.

Chapter 10
Episode One

In the years since *Return of the Jedi*, Star Wars had never really gone away. In 1978, George oversaw the publication of *Splinter of the Mind's Eye*, a novel by Alan Dean Foster that took place in the Star Wars universe. In 1987, West End Games introduced a role-playing game. The games filled in details about the universe that George approved and then handed over to other writers. In 1991, Timothy Zahn wrote *Heir to the Empire*, and the book kicked off a new wave of Star Wars

enthusiasm. More books followed. By the time George announced his plans to make more Star Wars movies, their universe had become bigger, more complex, and even more beloved.

The three new movies George planned were prequels, the action taking place *before* the stories in the earlier films. To finance the new films, he decided to rerelease the original trilogy in theaters.

Hollywood was skeptical. Why would people buy tickets for old movies? The first three had come out twenty years earlier. All had already been shown on television. But once again, Hollywood was wrong. Fans waited on long lines to see them again. Many adults who had loved the movies as kids were now taking their own children to see *Star Wars*. People brought their old lightsabers.

THE PEOPLE VS. GEORGE LUCAS

THE 1997 RELEASES WERE DIFFERENT FROM THE ORIGINALS. GEORGE HAD CLEANED UP THE PRINTS OF THE FILMS AND ADDED MORE SPECIAL EFFECTS. IN SOME PLACES HE'D TWEAKED THE STORY. NOT ALL FANS WERE HAPPY WITH THE CHANGES. BUT AS FAR AS GEORGE WAS CONCERNED, THESE "IMPROVED" VERSIONS WERE THE *ONLY* ONES. HE HAD NO PLANS TO RELEASE THE MOVIES IN THEIR ORIGINAL FORM ON DVD. MANY PEOPLE FELT HE WAS TAKING AWAY MOVIE HISTORY AND CHANGING THE WORK OF OTHER PEOPLE, LIKE THE ORIGINAL SPECIAL-EFFECTS CRAFTSMEN. FANS ARGUED THEIR CAUSE PASSIONATELY ON THE INTERNET. THEY HAD GROWN UP WITH THE STAR WARS MOVIES. THEY WERE SUCH AN IMPORTANT PART OF FANS' LIVES, THEY FELT THE MOVIES BELONGED TO THEM IN A SPECIAL WAY, AND THEY DIDN'T WANT THEM CHANGED.

MANY FANS OVER THE YEARS HAVE EVEN MADE THEIR OWN FILM AND VIDEO TRIBUTES. GEORGE HAS ALWAYS ENCOURAGED THEIR CREATIVITY, EVEN MAKING THE OFFICIAL MOVIE SOUND EFFECTS AVAILABLE ONLINE. IN 2010, A DOCUMENTARY EXAMINED THE ARGUMENT FROM BOTH SIDES. AS THE CREATOR OF STAR WARS, GEORGE BELIEVES

THE MOVIES BELONG TO HIM, TO CHANGE AND
ADAPT IN WHATEVER WAYS HE FEELS ARE BEST.

Star Wars was rereleased on January 31, 1997. *Empire* was released three weeks later, and *Jedi* three weeks after that. The films topped the box office once again, earning $138 million, $67 million, and $45 million, respectively.

On May 19, 1999, the first of the prequels, *Star*

Wars: Episode I—The Phantom Menace, opened in theaters. This time, no one was surprised when it broke box office records. It spawned popular video games like *Star Wars: Episode I—Racer*, which let players pod-race like young Anakin in the movie. *Phantom Menace* was followed in 2002 by *Attack*

of the Clones, and *Revenge of the Sith* in 2005. George directed all three films himself, and his children appeared in small roles.

The three prequels tell the story of how Luke's father, Anakin Skywalker, became first a Jedi hero and then, tragically, the evil Darth Vader, who is the villain of the original trilogy. In the first film, *The Phantom Menace,* Anakin is a ten-year-old slave on Luke's home planet of Tatooine. The actor Hayden Christensen portrayed Anakin as a young man in the second film, *Attack of the Clones.* As a boy, Hayden had played at being a Jedi Knight with his friends. The first time a fight scene was filmed for the movie, George had to remind Hayden not to make the lightsaber noises himself as he had done as a young boy!

Some characters from the original trilogy appear as their younger selves. Obi-Wan was played by Ewan McGregor, whose uncle had appeared in all three original movies as pilot

Wedge Antilles. R2-D2 and C-3PO also appear, as do the child Boba Fett and a younger, swashbuckling Yoda.

The last movie, *Revenge of the Sith*, ends with the birth of Luke and Leia and the death of their mother, the heroic Padmé Amidala.

The movies were followed by the hugely popular animated TV show *Star Wars: The Clone Wars*.

In 2012, George became engaged to Mellody Hobson, who was working for Steven Spielberg's film company, DreamWorks. Mellody said she knew right away that George was "the one" for her, but they dated for years before George popped the question. When he did, he admitted he'd been carrying around the ring for six months.

They married in Beverly Hills in 2013.

By then, George had announced he was selling
Lucasfilm to the Walt Disney Corporation for
$4.05 billion. "It's now time for me to pass Star
Wars on to a new generation of filmmakers,"
he said. Disney announced that a new Star
Wars movie would be released in 2015 with
Mark Hamill, Carrie Fisher, and Harrison Ford
appearing as their original characters.

In August 2013, Everest Hobson Lucas, George and Mellody's daughter, was born. Would George finally retire? Probably not. With Skywalker Ranch he brought to life the idea he had originally imagined for American Zoetrope: an independent movie studio far from Hollywood. Through Lucasfilm, ILM, and Skywalker Sound, George Lucas has continued to change and influence the way movies are made.

Nobody knows what George Lucas will do next, but whatever it is, the Force will certainly be with him.

TIMELINE OF
GEORGE LUCAS'S LIFE

1944	George Lucas is born in Modesto, California
1962	George nearly dies in a car accident
1966	George graduates from USC
1967	George wins the top prize at the National Student Film Festival for *Electronic Labyrinth: THX 1138 4EB*
1969	George marries Marcia Lucas
1971	The feature-film version of *THX 1138* is released
1973	*American Graffiti* is released
1975	George founds Industrial Light and Magic
1977	*Star Wars* is released
1981	*Raiders of the Lost Ark* is released George and Marcia Lucas adopt daughter Amanda
1983	George and Marcia Lucas divorce
1988	George adopts daughter Katie ILM creates the first morphing sequence for *Willow*
1992	George receives the Irving G. Thalberg Memorial Award
1993	George adopts son Jett
1999	*The Phantom Menace* is released
2002	*Attack of the Clones* is released
2005	*Revenge of the Sith* is released The American Film Institute gives George a Life Achievement Award
2012	The Walt Disney Corporation buys Lucasfilm
2013	George marries Mellody Hobson Daughter Everest is born

TIMELINE OF
THE WORLD

The Ark of the Covenant disappears from the Temple of Jerusalem	587 BC (APPROX.)
The last Crusade ends	1272
T. E. Lawrence helps Arab forces capture Aqaba	1917
The Milky Way chocolate bar is created	1923
The Jazz Singer, the first feature-length movie with sound, is released	1927
The first rocket is launched into space from Germany	1942
The Korean War starts	1950
The Cuban revolution begins	1953
President Richard Nixon visits China	1972
The first pictures are taken of the planet Mars	1976
Hostages are taken at the American Embassy in Iran	1979
A failed assassination attempt is made on Pope John Paul II	1981
An explosion occurs at the Chernobyl Nuclear Power Plant in Ukraine	1986
Diana, Princess of Wales, dies	1997
Facebook is launched	2004
The Arab Spring, a wave of demonstrations and protests in the Middle East, begins	2010
South Korean singer Psy's "Gangnam Style" video goes viral	2012
Scientists construct a 3-D printer that can create material very similar to human tissue	2013

BIBLIOGRAPHY

* Carrau, Bob. **Monsters and Aliens from George Lucas**. New York: Harry N. Abrams, 1993.

Hearn, Markus. **The Cinema of George Lucas.** New York: Harry N. Abrams, 2005.

Kaminski, Michael. "In Tribute to Marcia Lucas," http://secrethistoryofstarwars.com/marcialucas.html.

* Kline, Sally, ed. *George Lucas:* **Interviews**. Jackson, MS: University Press of Mississippi, 1999.

The People vs. George Lucas, directed by Alexandre O. Philippe. Distributed by Exhibit A Pictures, Quark Films, 2010.

* Pollock, Dale. **Skywalking: The Life and Films of George Lucas**. New York: Da Capo Press, 1999.

Rubin, Michael. **Droidmaker: George Lucas and the Digital Revolution**. Gainesville, FL: Triad Publishing, 2006.

* White, Dana. **George Lucas**. Minneapolis: Lerner Publications, 2000.

* Books for young readers